The Chaos of Catechism

Finding Clarity in and Navigating the Call to Serve, Preach, Shepherd, and Evangelize

Hamin Chamberlain

Contents

Dedication

I dedicate this book to the life and legacy of my grandmother, Gertrude Thomas-Chamberlain. (1/7/1936-10/22/2019).

She was more than the foundation of our family; she was the heartbeat that kept us together. Her prayers rose like incense in the morning, and her wisdom was a steady lamp in the dark.

She taught me that faith was not simply something to be spoken, but something to be lived day after day, trial after trial, blessing after blessing. Her kitchen table was a pulpit; her life was a lesson, and her example was a sermon without words. She poured into me the value of hard work, the necessity of humility, and the beauty of serving others with grace. Even when her body grew tired, her spirit remained strong, and her love never wavered. Though she now rests in the eternal arms of the Father, her voice still echoes in my heart. I can still hear her laughter, still recall her encouragement, and still feel her prayers covering me in moments of weakness. This book is not only a tribute to her memory, but also an offering of gratitude for the seeds she planted. Seeds of faith, courage, and endurance that continue to bear fruit in my life.

Grandmom, this is for you. May every word on these pages reflect the lessons you taught me, and may your legacy live on in the lives of all who read them.

I love you forever, "Old Lady"

Acknowledgements

To my family, firstly my mother, Lisa Yvette Chamberlain, then to my uncles, cousins, and close friends: thank you for standing with me and for simply being my people. Your love and support have been the steady ground beneath my feet and will continue to be so.

To my foundational spiritual influences, Bishop Gilbert Coleman, Jr., and Rashiid K. Coleman. I must say thank you. Thank you for the many years of instilling in me foundational truths, challenging me and reminding me always to BE THE VALUE.

To my current pastor, Supt. Jerome Barmore, thank you for believing in me and opening the door to walk into my NEXT. And finally, to every leader…aspiring and solidified, both present and future, holding this book in your hands: this work is for you.

About the Author

Hamin Chamberlain is a native of Philadelphia, Pennsylvania, and an Ordained Elder in the Church of God in Christ. His road into ministry has been anything but traditional, yet that very journey fuels his passion: to equip future leaders with the guidance he once wished he had. His story is one of grace, persistence, and discovery all proof that God's call does not always follow predictable patterns, but it always finds its mark.

He attended University City High School, an institution that no longer exists, which in some ways made him feel like a nomad. In those days, he was searching for a sense of belonging beyond what he had already been blessed with a search that now compels him to help others who feel, or will one day feel, the same way. Licensed in 2018 and later ordained as an elder in 2020, Hamin is quite literally "just getting started." Yet his rearing from childhood into his late twenties deeply prepared him for ministry, even when he had no idea what and if something like this would ever come. Those formative years, both inside and outside the church, shaped the compassion and conviction that now mark his ministry.

In ministry, Hamin has a unique ability to intertwine "stories," and occurrences, into his messages at the same time flowing with practical insights to deliver the message of Jesus, our Christ. He preaches and serves within his local church (when called upon) while also carrying the Word beyond its walls as doors of opportunity have opened. His voice carries the weight of lived experience, coupled with the perspective of someone who knows what it means to be shaped in hidden seasons before being released into public ones. A communicator at heart,

Hamin is also expanding his ministry to digital platforms, creating an online space designed to encourage, teach, and inspire people right where they are. Through short teachings, motivational content, and practical lessons, he looks to meet a generation hungry for hope yet often disconnected from the traditional church. His vision is to help believers and leaders alike move from confusion to clarity, from doubt to courage, and from chaos to calling. And that has spawned into a major faith move, for him personally. As he will be revamping and launching his social media (Facebook, Instagram, TikTok) as online ministry platforms. In the winter of 2026.

Beyond ministry, Hamin is passionate about all thing's sports, from the NFL, WNBA, and NBA to tennis. He loves cooking (and is great at it), traveling, spending time with family, and kicking it with friends. He is just as comfortable vibing out on his own with a good movie and great music.

These everyday joys keep him grounded, reminding him that ministry is lived not only in the pulpit but in the rhythms of ordinary life. Through every role that he holds whether it be elder, preacher, writer, encourager, builder, or family man, Hamin's heart beats with one desire: to see others walk boldly and faithfully into the call of God in their lives.

The Chaos of Catechism is his first book, but it will not be his last contribution to the kingdom. For Hamin, writing is simply another avenue to serve, another way to teach, shepherd, and equip the people of God for the work and way ahead.

Introduction

Stepping into ministry is one of the most rewarding and one of the most daunting journeys a believer can take.

Though some traditions have historically limited these offices to men, it is vital to state clearly that this book was written for both men and women. The call to serve, preach, shepherd, and evangelize is not confined by or to gender. Throughout history, God has raised up women alongside men to carry His message, lead His people, and embody His kingdom. This is not a book that perpetuates exclusion; it is a book that celebrates the fullness of God's call to all who will choose to answer.

For centuries, churches have practiced some form of catechism: a process of teaching, testing, and preparing candidates for entering ministry. While the word may sound old-fashioned, the experience is timeless. It is a season filled with questions, expectations, doubts, and at times, chaos. And yet, in that chaos, God is shaping something powerful. He is chiseling character. He is refining motives. He is teaching us that ministry is not built on titles or positions but on the bedrock of service, obedience, and most importantly, love. The catechism process is less about passing a test and more about being tested by the journey.

Every person who accepts the call soon realizes the weight of it. A call to ministry is not simply an invitation to "do church work," it is a summons, a clarion call to live differently, to think differently, to be different, and to surrender in ways that stretch the very soul. Deacons are called to serve with humility. Ministers are charged to preach with boldness. Elders are entrusted to guard and guide flocks. Evangelists are sent to carry the gospel beyond the walls, into streets, neighborhoods, nations, and to generations. Each office is unique, yet each is vital to the health and growth of the church. It is my belief that together, they form the backbone of spiritual leadership, ensuring that the message of Christ not only survives but thrives.

This book has been designed with this thought in mind: to bring clarity in the middle of that chaos. It is not a denominational handbook, nor does it claim to answer every theological nuance. Instead, the goal is to provide a practical overview of the four primary offices many believers encounter in their preparation for ministry: Deacons, Ministers, Elders, and Evangelists. My aim is not to bog you down with rigid formulas but to give you handles, clear truths, and principles you can hold onto when the waters and weight of ministry begin to feel overwhelming.

I write with this conviction: that God has not called you to confusion, but to clarity; not to burnout, but to balance; not to status, but to servanthood. While some traditions emphasize these roles differently, the principles of service, stewardship, and evangelism remain constant across the body of Christ at large. They are truths that transcend denominations, cultures, and generations. They apply to both men and women who embrace the call of ministry, because the call of God is no respecter of persons.

Perhaps you are a candidate preparing for ordination, nervously awaiting the laying on of hands. Or you are a leader tasked with guiding others through the process, remembering your own journey as you pour into theirs. Or you are simply a believer curious about the roles within the church, eager to understand why these offices matter and how they function in the life of the body. Wherever you may find yourself, this book will provide you with insight, encouragement, and tools for the journey ahead.

And let me be clear: this is more than information. My earnest prayer is that as you turn these pages, something deeper awakens in you, that you will not only understand the responsibilities of each office but also embrace the spirit behind them: the heart of a servant, the hands of a steward, and the fire of an evangelist. My hope is that you will finish this book with more than head knowledge but that you will finish with a renewed hunger to serve Christ with excellence, integrity, and passion.

So, take a breath. Lean in. Let us navigate the chaos together, and in the process, discover the clarity God has been waiting to reveal.

Chapter 1:
The Deacon- Servants of the Church

Greatness through Service

"The greatest among you will be your servant"

Matthew 23:11

The Calling of a Deacon

In many congregations today, deacons may oversee benevolence ministries, food pantries, or financial stewardship. The small, quiet acts, groceries delivered to a struggling family, bills paid for a widow, transportation arranged for the elderly, are echoes of Stephen's ministry. These moments rarely make headlines, but they uphold the credibility of the church's witness.

And this is a mirror of the model that we saw in ancient times:

When the early church began to grow rapidly, the apostles faced a problem: the needs of the people were outpacing the leadership's capacity to serve them all. In Acts 6, we read of widows being overlooked in the daily distribution of food. Rather than neglect prayer and the ministry of the Word, the apostles appointed seven men, full of the Spirit and wisdom, to oversee these practical matters. This was the birth of the office of the deacon. The Greek word used in Acts 6 is diakonos (διάκονος), meaning servant, minister, attendant. It carries the imagery of someone who stirs up dust while running an errand- in other words, a person so eager to serve that movement and action follow them. From the beginning, deacons were not chosen simply because they had time, money, or a good reputation in the community. They were chosen because they carried spiritual maturity, humility, and faithfulness. Their role was not lesser than that of the apostles! It was different, but equally essential.

Principle: The calling of a deacon is not about filling a gap; it is about embodying the heart of Christ, who Himself declared, *"I am among you as one who serves"* (Luke 22:27).

A Deacon in Action: Stephen

One of those seven chosen was Stephen. Scripture calls him *"a man full of faith and of the Holy Spirit" (Acts 6:5).* While Stephen was appointed to serve tables, his ministry did not stop there. He performed great wonders and signs among the people, and his wisdom was so Spirit-filled that even those who opposed him could not stand against him.

Stephen eventually became the church's first martyr, boldly testifying of Christ before the council in Acts 7. His life teaches us two important truths about being a deacon:

Have you ever heard of the term, there is no such thing as BIG I's and little You's? Well, my friends…it is undoubtedly true.

1. No role is "small" in God's kingdom. Serving tables positioned Stephen to be a witness before rulers.

2. Every act of service is spiritual. Though his role was practical, Stephen was empowered by the Spirit in all he said and did.

Stephen's ministry demonstrates to us that the Spirit makes no distinction between those who serve at tables and those who stand behind pulpits. Faithful service unlocks spiritual authority. His miracles were not divorced from his service but flowed out of it. The one who proved he was faithful with bread became a vessel through which the Bread of Life was proclaimed.

Practical Application: Modern deacons may not distribute food daily, but they carry the same Spirit-driven mandate, which is to see every task, whether administrative, financial, or logistical, as an act of worship unto the Lord. Deacons, therefore, are not "helpers in the shadows." They are spiritual leaders who model faith, courage, and service in some of the most powerful ways.

The Hands of Compassion

The role of a deacon can be understood in three parts:

1. Service to People– meeting practical needs with humility and compassion. The Greek nuance of diakonia highlights not just action, but service motivated by love.

2. Support for Leadership– freeing pastors and elders to focus on prayer and teaching. This is not subordination but partnership, enabling the Word to spread without distraction.

3. Stewardship– caring for resources entrusted to the church faithfully and wisely. This includes finances, property, and even the church's reputation in the community.

These three (3) components of the office can create what is called:

The Sheepdog Perspective

Shepherds are called to feed and lead the flock, but they cannot do it alone. In the natural world, shepherds rely on sheepdogs (loyal, alert, and tireless helpers) to guard the sheep, keep them from wandering, and chase away predators. The sheepdog does not replace the shepherd, nor does it take credit for the flock's well-being. Instead, it faithfully aids, ensuring the shepherd can focus on guiding the flock.

In the same way, deacons function as sheepdogs in the church:

Protectors of Peace: Deacons often stand at the "edges" of the congregation, sensing unrest, mediating conflict, and ensuring no one is overlooked or left behind (Acts 6).

Watchmen Against Division: Like sheepdogs circling the flock, deacons help prevent murmuring from festering into division, just as Stephen and the other six safeguarded unity by caring for the neglected widows.

Supporters of Shepherds: Deacons do not seek the spotlight. Instead, they help shoulder burdens so pastors and elders can give themselves fully to prayer and the Word (Acts 6:4).

Guardians of the Vulnerable: A sheepdog instinctively protects the weakest in the flock. Likewise, deacons are often the first to notice a widow struggling, a family in need, or a new believer drifting, and they innately step in with compassion and care. A good sheepdog is not praised for its bark or bite, but for its loyalty to the shepherd and attentiveness to the sheep. So too, faithful deacons gain no glory for themselves, they instead point all honor back to Christ, the Chief Shepherd.

Principle of note: A church with strong deacons is a church where both spiritual and practical needs are met, creating space for growth and unity.

I am sure there have been times in church that many of you, as have I, heard someone in a microphone talking about "heart posture."

With that thought in mind, let's dive into:

The Heart of a Deacon

The qualifications of a deacon in 1 Timothy 3 remind us that the role is more about character than skill. Deacons are to be worthy of respect, sincere, not indulging in much wine, and not pursuing dishonest gain. They must keep hold of the deep truths of the faith and exercise clear conscience.

Greek Insight: The phrase *"not double-tongued"* (1 Timothy 3:8) comes from the word dilogos (δίλογος), meaning two words, or speaking out of both sides of the mouth. This should always be a reminder to us that integrity in speech is a sure-fire non-negotiable.

It was the legendary former leader of Duke Men's Basketball team, Coach Mike Krzyzewski aka Coach K., who said during a most recent Q&A...that "he'd much rather have individuals who are talented and have character, then a group of talented characters."

In short, we must come to the realization that gifting and skill are not substantial enough. A deacon's life must mirror the message they support. Their authority is not positional but moral and spiritual, rooted in credibility and character.

Challenges to Anticipate:

1. ***Serving Without Recognition***– *much of a deacon's work or service in general is often dirty work that goes expected, yet at the same time unappreciated, and unseen, but never unnoticed by God.*

2. ***Balancing Authority–*** *deacons support leadership, not replace it. This requires humility and clarity of role.*

3. ***Guarding Against Burnout–*** *practical service can be exhausting; spiritual renewal through prayer and The Word is essential. It is your lifeline.*

Tips for Preparation:

1. Maintain a Devotional Life– intimacy with God fuels effective service.

2. Study Scripture– the Word equips deacons for wise decisions and encouragement.

3. Grow in Discernment– sensitivity to the Spirit helps deacons serve wisely in difficult situations.

4. Cultivate Practical Skills– organization, communication, and problem-solving strengthen ministry impact.

Principle & Practice: The deacon's preparation is both spiritual and practical- filled with prayer and Scripture but also sharpened by anointing and skills that meet real needs.

Reflection Questions– Chap. 1: The Deacon

1. What is the biblical origin of the deacon role, and how did it emerge in Acts 6?

_____

_____

_____

2. List at least three qualifications of a deacon from 1 Timothy 3. Why are these significant?

_____

_____

_____

3. What does the Greek word diakonos mean, and how does its meaning shape our understanding of the deacon's role?

_____

_____

_____

4.   Why did the apostles appoint deacons instead of handling every practical need themselves? What does this teach us about leadership and delegation?

_____

_____

_____

5.   How does the role of a deacon support and strengthen the work of pastors and elders?

_____

_____

_____

6.   Why is character emphasized more than skill in the qualifications of a deacon?

_____

_____

_____

7.   In your own words, explain the difference between "serving tables" and "preaching the Word." Why does the church need both?

_____

_____

_____

8.   Stephen is described as "full of faith and the Holy Spirit." What lessons can we draw from his service and his bold witness?

_____

_____

_____

9.   Scenario: A church member approaches you, saying their family has no food for the week. How should a deacon respond, both practically and spiritually?

_____

_____

_____

10. What spiritual disciplines are especially important for a deacon to cultivate, and why?

_____

_____

_____

11. How can a deacon guard against pride, burnout, or power struggles while serving in leadership?

_____

_____

_____

12. In what way(s) can the ministry of a deacon impact the unity and growth of a local church?

_____

_____

_____

13. How do you respond when your service goes unnoticed? What does this reveal about your heart?

_____

_____

_____

14. Reflect personally: What draws you to the role of a deacon, and how do you see yourself living out servant leadership in your own context?

_____

_____

_____

Closing Thought:

The deacon embodies Christ's model of leadership through service. To serve as a deacon is to walk in the footsteps of the One who washed feet, fed multitudes, and laid down His own life. It is to say, with every act of service, *"Not to us, Lord, not to us, but to Your name be the glory"* (Psalm 115:1).

The role of a deacon is not about titles, recognition, or power. It is about servanthood. In a world that often chases status, the deacon quietly models the heart of Christ, who came not to be served, but to serve.

If you are preparing to step into this office, embrace the calling with joy. You may never stand behind a pulpit every Sunday, but you will hold a vital place in the kingdom of God: a servant who helps keep the body of Christ healthy, strong, and whole.

"God is not unjust; he will not forget your work and the love you have shown him as you have helped his people and continue to help them." Hebrews 6:10.

Chapter 2:
The Minister– Carriers of the Word

The Charge to Remember

"Preach the word; be prepared in season and out of season; correct, rebuke, and encourage with great patience and careful instruction."

-2 Timothy 4:2

The Calling of a Minister

Where deacons are primarily called to serve tables, ministers are called to carry the Word. The office of a minister is often the first visible step into pulpit ministry, but it extends far beyond public speaking.

The term minister finds its root in the Latin ministerium, meaning service or office of service. In the New Testament, two Greek words help us grasp its depth. The first is diakonos (διάκονος), which we encountered in Chapter 1 a servant, one who waits on others. The second is leitourgos (λειτουργός), meaning public servant or one who serves for the benefit of the people. This word carries the sense of someone appointed to an official duty, often in worship or public service.

In the Hebrew Scriptures, the closest concept is sharat (שָׁרַת) meaning to minister, to serve, or to attend. This word describes how Joshua ministered to Moses (Exodus 24:13), how Samuel ministered before the Lord as a boy (1 Samuel 2:11), and how the priests served before God in the tabernacle.

Taken together, these words paint a consistent picture: a minister is not someone who stands above others, but one who stands before God on behalf of others. Ministry is intercession and proclamation, service at the altar of God and service to the people of God.

Principle: To be a minister is not simply to have a title, but it is to accept the weight of representing God's Word faithfully, and to live in such a way that both your lips and your life proclaim Christ.

Let us pivot and examine:

The Role of a Minister

The role of a minister can vary by denomination, but the heart of ministry remains consistent: serving God's people and carrying His Word with faithfulness and integrity. Ministers are entrusted with sacred responsibilities that extend beyond titles or ceremonies. Most responsibilities you will find fall under these categories:

1.   Preaching & Teaching: Ministers communicate the Word of God with clarity and truth. Their task is not to entertain or to impress but to explain and apply Scripture so that the church may grow in wisdom and maturity.

2. Assisting in Worship & Sacraments:

Ministers help lead prayer, administer communion or baptism, and guide worship gatherings. These acts are not simply rituals, but reminders of God's covenant with His people. Whether standing behind the communion table or leading a congregation in prayer, ministers point hearts toward Christ, the true High Priest.

3. Pastoral Support: Ministers share in shepherding duties: visiting the sick, counseling the weary, comforting the grieving, and leading outreach efforts. This role reflects the compassion of Christ, who saw the crowds as sheep without a shepherd (Mark 6:34). In these moments, ministry is often less about words and more about presence.

Personal Example: Ministers are called to live as embodied sermons. Paul told Timothy: "Set an example for the believers in speech, in conduct, in love, in faith and in purity" (1 Timothy 4:12). A minister's greatest sermon is not always the one preached on Sunday, but the one lived on Monday. Integrity, humility, and consistency in daily life give credibility to every message delivered from the pulpit.

Anchor Point: The role of a minister is both public and private! Seen in preaching and worship leadership, but proven in hospital rooms, living rooms, and in the quiet choices of everyday life.

The Heart of a Minister

Paul's letters to Timothy and Titus serve as training manuals for ministers. In them, we see not just a job description, but a spiritual blueprint. A minister is called to embody the following:

- **Diligence in the Word**– "Do your best to present yourself to God as one approved, a worker who does not need to be ashamed and who correctly divides the word of truth" (2 Timothy 2:15). Ministers must be students before they are teachers, feeding others only after they themselves have been nourished by the Word. Their authority comes not from personality, but from Scripture faithfully taught.

- **Endurance Under Pressure**– Ministry is not for the faint of heart. Paul admonishes Timothy to "endure hardship like a good soldier of Christ Jesus" (2 Timothy 2:3). Ministers will face misunderstandings, criticism, and even opposition but they must remain steady. The measure of a minister is not seen in easy seasons, but in how they stand when the storms come.

- **Purity of Life**– Character validates calling. "Watch your life and doctrine closely. Persevere in them, because if you do, you will save both yourself and your hearers" (1 Timothy 4:16). A minister's integrity is the bridge that carries their message into the hearts of others. Without it, even the best sermons can fall flat.

- **Faithfulness to the Call**– Ministry is not a hobby or side pursuit; it is a sacred trust. Paul reminds Timothy to "fan into flame the gift of God" (2 Timothy 1:6). Ministers are stewards of something holy not to be taken lightly, not to be abandoned when it becomes inconvenient, but carried with loyalty until the end.

Truth to Carry Forward:

The heart of a minister is measured not in eloquence, but in endurance; not in charisma, but in character; not in titles, but in a life faithfully surrendered to the call of God.

Challenges to Anticipate

- **Finding Your Voice**– Every minister begins by learning from others, but true effectiveness comes when you discover the voice God has given you. Paul reminded the Corinthians, "Our competence comes from God" (2 Corinthians 3:5). Authentic preaching flows not from imitation, but from intimacy with the Lord.

- **Handling Criticism**– Ministers who preach truth must expect resistance. Some criticism is unfair; some are necessary corrections both must be handled with humility and resilience. Paul encouraged Timothy to "endure hardship" (2 Timothy 2:3), knowing that opposition is part of the calling.

- **Balancing Zeal with Wisdom**– Passion is a gift, but unrestrained zeal can wound rather than heal. Paul confessed to his fellow Israelites, "They are zealous for God, but their zeal is not based on knowledge" (Romans 10:2). A wise minister learns to pair fire with wisdom, passion with patience.

- **Maintaining Personal Devotion**– It is possible to preach while spiritually running on empty. A minister who does not guard their private walk will soon falter in public ministry. Jesus Himself often withdrew to lonely places to pray (Luke 5:16), modeling for us the rhythm of pouring out and being refilled.

Wisdom for the Journey:

Challenges in ministry are not signs of disqualification but opportunities for growth. Each trial presses the minister deeper into dependence on God, shaping endurance, humility, and maturity.

Tips for Preparation:

1. **Deepen Your Study Life**: Scripture must live in you before you preach it. Paul told Timothy, "Devote yourself to the public reading of Scripture, to preaching and to teaching" (1 Timothy 4:13). A minister cannot pour out what they have not first absorbed. Make time for both academic study and devotional reading so the Word shapes your head and your heart.

2. Master Sermon Structure: Preaching is both art and discipline. Practice writing and delivering short messages that are clear, biblical, and Christ-centered. Like Apollos in Acts 18, who was "mighty in the Scriptures," ministers should grow in skill so that their message can be heard without distraction.

3. Learn from Mentors: Every minister needs voices of wisdom to guide them. Sit under seasoned pastors, ask questions, and welcome corrections. Timothy had Paul; Elisha had Elijah; Joshua had Moses. Ministry is not mastered in isolation but through apprenticeship and accountability.

4. Keep a Servant's Heart: The pulpit is not a stage it is an altar. Ministers are not performers but servants who point people to Christ. Jesus Himself washed His disciples' feet, showing us that true authority flows from humility. The higher the calling, the deeper the posture of service must be.

Lesson in Action:

Preparation is more than sermon notes it is shaping a life that reflects Christ. A minister prepares not just to preach well, but to live well before God and His people.

A Minister in Action:

Timothy

When we think of ministers in Scripture, Timothy stands out as a prime example. Paul called him his "true son in the faith" (1 Timothy 1:2) and entrusted him with responsibilities far beyond his age. Timothy was young, timid at times, and often needed encouragement yet Paul reminded him: "Don't let anyone look down on you because you are young, but set an example for the believers in speech, in conduct, in love, in faith and in purity" (1 Timothy 4:12).

The name Timothy means "honoring God." His life reflected that meaning, even when he wrestled with fear and insecurity. Paul urged him to "fan into flame the gift of God" (2 Timothy 1:6), teaching us that courage is not the absence of fear but faithfulness in the face of it.

From Timothy's life we learn that:

1. Ministry is not limited by age or background. God equips whom He calls, regardless of human expectations.

2. Mentorship matters. Timothy's ministry was shaped by Paul's guidance, correction, and encouragement. Every minister needs spiritual parents who will invest in them.

3. Example outweighs eloquence. A minister's life preaches even louder than their sermons. Integrity is the platform from which true ministry is heard.

Timothy's journey reassures every new minister: you do not have to have it all figured out on day one. What matters most is faithfulness, teachability, and devotion to God's Word.

Key Takeaway:

Like Timothy, ministers are called to grow into their calling not by striving for perfection, but by walking daily in faith, humility, and obedience.

Ministers Mirror:

1. What is the Hebrew word for "minister," and what does it mean?

_____

_____

_____

2. What Greek word is often translated "minister," and what does it emphasize?

_____

_____

_____

3. According to 2 Timothy 4:2, what are ministers commanded to do?

_____

_____

_____

4. Why must a minister "rightly divide the Word of truth"?

_____

_____

_____

5. Name at least two responsibilities of a minister outside of preaching.

_____

_____

_____

6. What qualities did Paul urge Timothy to model for believers in 1 Timothy 4:12?

_____

_____

_____

7. Scenario: You are asked to preach with only a few hours' notice. How would you prepare spiritually and practically?

_____

_____

_____

8. How should a minister manage criticism after delivering a sermon?

_____

_____

_____

9. What dangers come from preaching zealously but without wisdom?

_____

_____

_____

10. Reflect personally: How do you guard your devotional life while preparing to pour out into others?

_____

_____

_____

11. Why is Timothy a good model for younger ministers stepping into leadership?

_____

_____

_____

12. How does Timothy's story show the importance of mentorship in ministry today?

_____

_____

_____

13. Who has been a "Paul" in your journey, and how are you preparing to be a "Paul" for someone else?

_____

_____

_____

14. What truth from this chapter will you be able to carry forward into your own ministry?

_____

_____

_____

Closing Thought:

The minister is not just a preacher they are a living servant of the Word. Their role is rooted in the ancient call to attend, serve, and represent God before His people. Whether teaching in a classroom, preaching in a pulpit, or praying with a hurting soul, the minister's task is the same: to carry the Word with faithfulness and humility.

If you are preparing for this office, anchor yourself in study, prayer, and purity of life. Remember: a minister may deliver many sermons in their lifetime, but their greatest sermon will always be the life they live.

"Watch your life and doctrine closely. Persevere in them, because if you do, you will save both yourself and your hearers." (1 Timothy 4:16)

Chapter 3:

The Elder– Guardians of the Flock

Shepherds of Willing Oversight

"Be shepherds of God's flock that is under your care, watching over them—not because you must, but because you are willing, as God wants you to be; not pursuing dishonest gain, but eager to serve."

-1 Peter 5:2.

The Calling of an Elder

The office of an elder is one of the highest callings within the church. While deacons serve tables and ministers carry the Word, elders guard the flock. They are entrusted with oversight, counsel, and spiritual governance.

In the New Testament, three words are often used to describe this role:

Presbyteros (πρεσβύτερος)– literally "older one." This highlights maturity and wisdom, not just in age but in tested faith.

Episkopos (ἐπίσκοπος)– often translated "overseer" or "bishop." It emphasizes responsibility, watchfulness, and accountability.

Poimēn (ποιμήν)– meaning "shepherd" or "pastor." This image captures care, protection, and guidance, reflecting Christ as the Good Shepherd.

Taken together, these words show that elders are not defined by charisma or popularity but by proven character and spiritual steadiness. Their calling is to lead not from a platform of personality but from a life of prayer, counsel, and faithful example.

Foundation to Build On:

We must always understand and operate from the thought of the elder's authority is not in title alone but in a life that demonstrates wisdom, maturity, and the heart of a shepherd.

The Elder vs. The Pastor- Distinctions & Overlap

The words elder, pastor, and bishop/overseer often appear in Scripture, sometimes interchangeably. Yet, when carefully studied, they highlight different dimensions of leadership in the life of the church. To blur them together without distinction is to miss the beauty of God's design.

Shared Ground- Shepherding Responsibility:

Both elders and pastors are called to shepherd the flock of God. Elders provide stability, accountability, and maturity; pastors labor in preaching, teaching, and daily care. Together, they ensure that the church is not merely inspired but also established.

Acts 20:28: Paul tells the Ephesian elders to "shepherd the church of God."

Elders are commanded to "feed the flock of God."

This means that both roles carry a shepherd's heart not driven by status, but by service.

Elders- Guardians of Maturity:

The Greek word presbyteros implies seasoned maturity, whether by age, wisdom, or proven faithfulness. Elders are the spiritual backbone of a congregation:

- They guard sound doctrine (Titus 1:9).

- They model godly character as examples for the flock (1 Peter 5:3).

- They provide counsel and correction when the body veers off course.

- Elders are less about "the microphone" and more about "the map." They ensure the church does not drift into error or instability.

Pastors- Shepherds of the Everyday:

The Greek word poimēn means "shepherd." Pastors embody the hands-on care of the local church:

- Feeding the flock through consistent preaching and teaching.

- Binding wounds through counseling, visitation, and encouragement.
- Leading the flock forward with vision and direction.

If elders provide framework, pastors provide fuel. One steadies the ship, the other drives it forward in a show of:

Shared Authority Under Christ

We know Christ as the true Head of the Church (Ephesians 5:23; Colossians 1:18). Both pastors and elders are under shepherds, not owners. Their authority is not about domination, but about stewardship. When they walk together, the church is protected from dictatorship on one hand, and disorder on the other.

Remember this...pastors shepherd the present, by carrying the "now"- the immediate needs, weekly gatherings, and the direction of the body.

The elder guards the long view- ensuring that the church remains faithful across generations.

Overlap- When Titles Intersect

In many New Testament passages, elders, overseers, and pastors appear as overlapping roles (Acts 20:17, 28; 1 Peter 5:1–2). This suggests that early church leadership was not a hierarchy of offices but a plurality of leaders who shared pastoral and teaching responsibilities.

Yet, in today's church culture, we often see the pastor as the visible leader and elders as the spiritual council. Both are biblical but the danger comes when one role overshadows the other.

When Balance Is Lost

- If a church has pastors without elders, it risks being visionary but unstable. Passion without accountability leads to burnout, false teaching, or abuse of power.

- If a church has elders without pastors, it risks being stable but stagnant. Tradition without fresh shepherding becomes lifeless and unengaging.

- But when pastors and elders walk in unity, the church becomes both deeply rooted and dynamically growing.

Practical Picture:

Think of a healthy church like a tree:

- The pastor is the gardener who waters, prunes, and tends daily.

- The elders are the deep roots that stabilize, nourish, and protect against storms.

- Together, they allow the tree (the congregation) to grow upward and outward without toppling over.

Biblical Models of Shepherding: Peter and Priscilla

Peter

Who was a fisherman by occupation, from Bethsaida. A job that clearly paints him already as a diligent worker. One being familiar with long nights, frustration, labor, but also persistence. We know Peter was not a wealthy man, nor highly educated like his soon to be counterpart (Paul)... (Acts 4) call him "unschooled and ordinary." This shines light on how God delights in using the "overlooked."

Peter embodied what many can see as a natural leader, or at the very least bold (among the 12, was always listed first).

Although a born leader Peter was not perfect. We remember his call (Luke 5), his confession (Matthew 16:13-20) but we cannot forget his shortcomings and denial (Luke 22:54-62).

After his restoration, Jesus charged Peter three times: "Shepherd my sheep" (John 21:16). Later, writing as an elder himself, Peter exhorted leaders to serve willingly, not domineering but being examples to the flock (1 Peter 5:1–3). His journey from impulsive fisherman to steady shepherd shows that eldership is not about perfection but transformation and leading with humility and grace.

A Lesson from Peter's Life:

An elder is forged, not born- We can see that peter had moments of instability that turned into steadfastness. And it was God who shaped him through failure, correction, and then the beauty of restoration.

Priscilla

Alongside her husband, Aquila were tentmakers. A notable and portable trade that allowed them to travel and establish themselves wherever the Gospel took them. They are first mentioned in Acts 18, after being expelled from Rome by Emperor Claudius, settled in Corinth. Priscilla guided the gifted preacher Apollos, "explaining to him the way of God more accurately" (Acts 18:26). Her wisdom and discernment reflect the teaching and guiding role elders provide in shaping others. She demonstrates that spiritual maturity and sound doctrine are essential marks of shepherding, whether in public or private settings.

Though cultural norms limited women's public teaching roles, Priscilla clearly exercised influence, and instruction in appropriate settings. Which highlights how spiritual maturity, not gender, was the qualifier for influence in the early church.

She was full of courage and shows great sacrifice as Paul says of them "they risked their lives" for him (Romans 16:4).

Priscilla was a **MODEL OF CONSISTENCY**. From Corinth to Ephesus to Rome, she shows up repeatedly. Ministry was not a phase for her; it was a lifelong devotion.

Key Takeaway: Eldership is modeled through both men and women who, empowered by the Spirit, guide, teach, and protect the flock with humility and wisdom.

The Shepherds Task...and The Charge of an Elder

Elders are guardians, protectors, and shepherds. Their role is weighty because it touches both doctrine and daily life. Four responsibilities stand out:

1. **Spiritual Oversight-** Like Peter, who warned the church to "be alert and of sober mind" (1 Peter 5:8), elders guard the flock against false teaching and spiritual danger. Oversight requires vigilance and courage.

2. **Pastoral Care-** Elders are called to be present in the needs of the people. Priscilla modeled this kind of care when she, alongside Aquila, guided Apollos privately and patiently, helping him grow without

shaming him publicly (Acts 18:26). Eldership means building up others with gentleness and discernment.

3. **Decision Making & Governance–** Elders, like the Jerusalem council in Acts 15 (where Peter and James both spoke), help steer the direction of the church with wisdom. Their decisions shape the unity and mission of the body.

4. **Modeling Christlike Leadership–** Peter exhorted: "Do not lord it over those entrusted to you but be examples to the flock" (1 Peter 5:3). Priscilla lived this too, showing that leadership is not domination but humble example.

Shepherd's Insight: Elders lead not by personality but by presence, guiding with wisdom and modeling Christlike care.

The Spirit of an Elder

Paul gives a clear standard in Titus 1:5–9: elders must be blameless, faithful to their spouse, hospitable, self-controlled, upright, holy, and disciplined. They must hold firmly to sound doctrine and be able to encourage others with it. These qualifications remind us that eldership is rooted in integrity more than ability, in maturity more than charisma.

Above all, an elder must carry a shepherding spirit. Leadership in this office is not about control, but care, not about prestige, but protection. Peter admonishes elders to lead "not because you must, but because you are willing... eager to serve" (1 Peter 5:2). And Priscilla modeled this same spirit when she and Aquila patiently taught Apollos, correcting him in private with grace and clarity (Acts 18:26).

Truth to Carry Forward: The spirit of an elder is seen not in how loudly they command, but in how faithfully they care. Guarding doctrine, guiding God's people, and reflecting the heart of the Chief Shepherd.

The Weight of Eldership

Leading Peers– Unlike ministers or deacons, elders often lead people who are their equals in age, status, or experience. This requires humility and wisdom. Peter, writing as a fellow elder (1 Peter 5:1), reminds us that eldership is not domination but servant leadership.

Confronting False Teaching: Elders must guard truth, even when it means standing against popular opinion. Paul warned the Ephesian elders that "savage wolves" would rise from among them (Acts 20:29–30). Priscilla offers a model here: correcting Apollos with both courage and grace (Acts 18:26).

Handling Conflict: Disputes will most assuredly arise within the flock, and elders must resolve them fairly and biblically. The Jerusalem council (Acts 15), where Peter played a leading role, shows how elders sought unity by appealing to Scripture and the Spirit's guidance.

Avoiding Spiritual Pride: With authority comes temptation. Elders must remember that they are still sheep under the Great Shepherd. Peter's words cut through this temptation: "All of you, clothe yourselves with humility toward one another, because 'God opposes the proud but shows favor to the humble'" (1 Peter 5:5).

Shepherd's Lense: Elders are not called to an easy path but to a faithful one that is marked by humility, courage, and a continual awareness that they serve under Christ, the Chief Shepherd.

Readiness for the Role

1. Immerse Yourself in Doctrine– Elders must know not only what they believe, but why it is they believe it. Paul urged Titus that an elder must "hold firmly to the trustworthy message" (Titus 1:9).

2. Develop Discernment– Learn to recognize spiritual attacks, false doctrine, and unhealthy patterns. Discernment is a safeguard for the flock.

3. Grow in Counseling Skills– Be prepared to listen, pray, and guide with gentleness and without biases. Much of the role of eldership is personal, not just public.

4. Pursue Accountability– Every elder needs other TRUSTED AND PROVEN leaders and peers to keep them grounded. Even Peter needed Paul to correct him (Galatians 2:11).

5. Cultivate Prayerfulness– Like the apostles in Acts 6, elders MUST prioritize prayer, interceding for the flock and for the wisdom in leadership decisions.

6. Practice Patience– Elders deal with people in all stages of growth. Patience reflects the long-suffering nature of the Chief Shepherd.

7. Strengthen Family Life– Paul tied eldership to the home: "If anyone does not know how to manage his own family, how can he take care of God's church?" (1 Timothy 3:5). Healthy and whole homes make healthy leaders.

Foundation to Build On: Readiness for eldership does not come from charisma or cleverness but from Christlike character, a life of prayer, faithfulness, and steady leadership.

The Elders Measure:

1. What three New Testament words are often used interchangeably for "elder," and what does each emphasize?

_____

_____

_____

2. In Acts 20:28–31, Paul charges elders to "keep watch" over the flock. What two dangers does he specifically warn against?

_____

_____

_____

3. According to Titus 1:5–9, list at least five qualifications of an elder. Why do these matter more than skill?

_____

_____

_____

4. What is the difference between leading by authority and leading by example?

_____

_____

_____

5. Scenario: A member of your church begins teaching doctrine that contradicts Scripture. As an elder, how would you address it biblically?

_____

_____

_____

6. Scenario: Two respected members are in sharp conflict, dividing the church. What steps should you take to reconcile them?

_____

_____

_____

7. Why is hospitality emphasized as a qualification for elders, and what does it look like in practice today?

_____

_____

_____

8. James 5:14 instructs elders to pray for the sick. How does this shape the elder's pastoral role?

_____

_____

_____

9. What dangers exist when elders neglect their own spiritual lives while caring for others?

_____

_____

_____

10. How does accountability among elders prevent pride or abuse of authority?

_____

_____

_____

11. Compare and contrast the roles of elders and deacons. Where do they overlap, and where do they differ?

_____

_____

_____

12. Personal Reflection: How do you balance being a shepherd to others while still being a sheep under Christ's care?

_____

_____

_____

Parting Word:

The office of an elder carries great weight and great responsibility. Elders are not only leaders but also guardians, protectors of truth, counselors of the hurting, and shepherds of the flock. Their calling is one of humility, integrity, and courage.

If you are preparing for this office, embrace the challenge with reverence. Remember: you are not just leading people—you are stewarding souls that belong to God and Him alone. Lead wisely, live purely, and guard the flock faithfully, until the Chief Shepherd appears.

"Now it is required that those who have been given a trust must prove faithful." -1 Corinthians 4:2

Chapter 4:
The Evangelist– Heralds of the
Gospel

The Evangelist's Mandate

"But you, keep your head in all situations, endure hardship, do the work of an evangelist, discharge all the duties of your ministry."

-2 Timothy 4:5

Evangelism is the engine that drives the church outward. Deacons serve, Ministers preach, Elders guard but Evangelists GO. And without going, the body risks turning inward instead of fulfilling the Great Commission.

The word evangelist comes from the Greek euangelistēs (εὐαγγελιστής), meaning one who announces good news. It is tied to euangelizō, to proclaim or announce the gospel.

An evangelist, then, is not just a preacher with a platform, but a messenger with a mission sent to break new ground, cross boundaries, and carry Christ where He has not yet been named.

Of all the offices, evangelism is in many ways the most vital, because it extends the reach of the kingdom. Without evangelists, the message would remain locked within the walls of the church. With evangelists, the gospel spreads across cities, nations, and generations.

Evangelists are the living echo of Christ's own mission: "The Son of Man came to seek and to save the lost" (Luke 19:10). To evangelize is not just to preach a message — it is to partner with heaven in the greatest rescue mission of all time.

Charge to Hold to:

Evangelism is not a side ministry of the church; it is the very heartbeat of the gospel, the outward thrust of God's saving love.

The Burden of the Evangelist:

Among the gifts Christ gave the church, evangelists hold a unique assignment (Ephesians 4:11). They are heralds. Those who publicly proclaim good news and compel people to respond. The Greek word euangelistēs (εὐαγγελιστής) literally means bringer of good news, and it is closely tied to the word kērux (κήρυξ), meaning herald or announcer. In the ancient world, a herald had one task: to faithfully deliver the king's message without alteration.

Evangelism *is not* an option for the church; it is the lifeline. Every believer is called to share their faith, but evangelists carry a special anointing to pierce hearts, draw crowds, and bring clarity to the gospel. Like Philip in Acts 8 or the Samaritan woman in John 4, evangelists are marked by urgency. They cannot stay silent because they understand eternity is always at stake.

Their ministry often involves bold proclamation in public spaces, personal witness in private conversations, and crossing cultural barriers to reach those far from God. They remind the church that the gospel is not meant to be contained but carried.

Truth to Carry Forward:

Evangelists embody the urgency of heaven, proclaiming Christ with passion, clarity, and conviction, knowing that every soul is of eternal worth.

Biblical Evangelists in Action:

Philip and the Samaritan Woman

Philip:

Philip, one of the seven deacons chosen in Acts 6, later emerges in Acts 8 as "Philip the Evangelist." When persecution scattered the believers, Philip went down to

Samaria and preached Christ. Entire crowds listened intently, miracles confirmed the message, and there was immense joy in the city.

Later, the Spirit led Philip to a desert road where he encountered the Ethiopian eunuch. Philip explained Isaiah 53, pointed him to Christ, and baptized him on the spot. That one encounter carried the gospel seed into another continent.

What we learn from Philip's ministry:

Evangelists MUST be:

1. Spirit-led, sensitive to divine appointments: The spirit gives the message power. The Gospel is not just mere words. It is "the power of God unto salvation" (Romans 1:16). Paul tells us that his preaching was not with "enticing words of man's wisdom, but in demonstration of the Spirit and of power" (1 Cor 2:4). Without the Spirit, even the clearest presentation can be absent of transformative power,

2. Bible-centered, ready to explain truth clearly: (Romans 10:17) reminds us, "Faith comes by hearing, and hearing by the Word of God." If the Word is not at the center, then faith cannot be produced.

3. People-focused, valuing one soul as much as an entire crowd: This is the *JESUS model*. Jesus constantly saw the person in the crowd. He noticed Zacchaeus in the tree, the blind beggar on the roadside. His compassion drove His mission (Matthew 9:36). Evangelists must follow His example which was loving people more than the spotlight.

4. Faithful to the message of the Gospel: An evangelist is not just a speaker, motivator, or crowd gatherer. Their core assignment is to faithfully proclaim the good news of Christ with clarity, conviction, and consistency. Everything else-charisma, boldness, and cultural awareness flows out of that root commitment to truth.

The Samaritan Woman:

In John 4, Jesus meets a Samaritan woman at a well. A woman doubly marginalized: first, as a Samaritan despised by Jews, and second, as one carrying a broken reputation. She came to the well at noon, avoiding the crowds, but instead encountered Christ.

In their conversation, Jesus revealed her past without condemnation and pointed her toward true worship: "God is spirit, and his worshipers must worship in the Spirit and in truth" (John 4:24). Her life was marked by thirst, shame, and rejection, yet in a single encounter she was transformed into a bold witness. Scripture says she left her water jar behind (John 4:28). That detail is powerful: the very object that symbolized her daily struggle and shame was abandoned because she had found living water. She ran into her city declaring: "Come, see a man who told me everything I ever did. Could this be the Messiah?" (John 4:29).

Her testimony stirred curiosity, drew people out of the city, and led multitudes to believe in Jesus. In fact, John 4:39 tells us: "Many of the Samaritans from that town believed in him because of the woman's testimony." What began as one private conversation became a public revival.

From the Samaritan woman's witness, we learn:

1. Evangelism is not about perfection, but it is about pointing people to Jesus. God can use even our most broken stories as testimonies of grace.

2. Your past does not disqualify you. In fact, it often amplifies your witness, showing the power of Christ to redeem.

3. Urgency matters. She wasted no time in telling her community what she had experienced. Real evangelism flows from real encounters.

4. Evangelism can break barriers. A woman once silenced became a voice that turned her whole community toward Christ.

The Endeavor of an Evangelist:

1. Proclaiming the Gospel: Evangelists specialize in preaching Christ crucified and risen with clarity and conviction. Paul declared: "We preach Christ crucified" (1 Corinthians 1:23). Whether Philip before crowds in Samaria or the Samaritan woman before her city, evangelists center the message on Jesus, not themselves.

2. Compelling the Lost: Evangelists carry a God-given urgency to call people to repentance and decision. Paul urged Timothy: "Do the work of an evangelist" (2 Timothy 4:5). Evangelists press for a response because they know eternity is always at stake.

3. Equipping the Church: Evangelists stir and train believers to share their faith, multiplying the harvest. Their presence ignites courage and conviction in the body, reminding the church that the Great Commission belongs to all. Like the Samaritan woman, whose testimony mobilized her whole community, evangelists spark others into action.

4. Crossing Boundaries: The evangelist breaks through barriers of culture, language, and tradition to bring the message wherever God sends them. Philip crossed into Samaria, breaking centuries of division; the Samaritan woman crossed social and gender expectations to proclaim Christ. True evangelism refuses to be confined by prejudice or fear.

The Evangelist's Insight: Evangelists extend the reach of the gospel by proclaiming, compelling, equipping, crossing, and carrying the message of Christ beyond walls, borders, and comfort zones.

The Essence of an Evangelist

Evangelists must live with urgency and endurance. Paul's charge to Timothy "do the work of an evangelist" (2 Timothy 4:5) still echoes today. Their heartbeat is not of comfort but of commission.

The Evangelist must hold true to:

- Resiliency under Hardship: Evangelists will face rejection, ridicule, and persecution. Paul told Timothy to "endure hardship" (2 Timothy 4:5). The Greek word makrothymia (long-suffering) captures the endurance required to keep preaching even when results are unseen.

- Focusing on Eternity: Every sermon, every conversation, every altar call is about rescuing souls from darkness to light.

- Living with a martyria (witness) that eternity is always at stake, and they cannot stay silent.

Charge to Remember: The heart of an evangelist beats with urgency, compassion, and endurance proclaiming Christ at any cost, until heaven is filled with those rescued from darkness.

The Hardships of the Herald

Carrying the gospel into new places is both glorious and costly. Evangelists are heralds of the King's message and heralds often face opposition before they see fruit. Paul's words still ring true: "Endure hardship, do the work of an evangelist" (2 Timothy 4:5).

Rejection: Many will not believe; some will resist fiercely. Jesus warned, "If they persecuted me, they would persecute you also" (John 15:20). Evangelists must learn to preach faithfully even when the response is silence or hostility.

Loneliness: Evangelists often travel and minister in unfamiliar places. Like Philip sent to a desert road, or Paul in foreign cities, heralds must find their strength in God's presence when human companionship is scarce.

Cultural Barriers: The gospel must be shared faithfully yet contextualized wisely. The Samaritan woman crossed cultural and gender boundaries with her testimony, showing that evangelists must navigate difference with wisdom and courage.

Spiritual Warfare: Evangelists confront the enemy head-on as they reclaim territory for Christ. Paul reminds us that "our struggle is not against flesh and blood" (Ephesians 6:12). Evangelists must fight on their knees before they fight with their words.

Anchor for Ministry: The hardships of the herald are real, but so is the reward. Evangelists endure rejection, loneliness, barriers, and warfare because they carry the King's message, and His Word never returns void.

Readiness for the Role:

1. Memorize Key Gospel Scriptures: Verses like John 3:16, Romans 10:9–10 and Acts 4:12 keep the message simple and clear. An evangelist must always be ready to proclaim Christ directly from the Word (2 Timothy 4:2).

2. Practice Your Testimony: Learn to share your story in three minutes or less. The Samaritan woman's entire witness boiled down to one sentence: "Come, see a man who told me everything I ever did" (John 4:29). Testimony is often the bridge to truth.

3. Study Apologetics Basics: Be prepared to answer objections like "Why Jesus?" or "Aren't all religions the same?" (1 Peter 3:15). Evangelists do not need to be philosophers, but they must be ready to defend the faith with clarity.

Foundation to Build On: Evangelism is both proclamation and incarnation. It is not only preaching the gospel with words but embodying the gospel with life.

Evangelists prepare not only by sharpening their words but by shaping their lives. Readiness flows from Scripture, Spirit, compassion, and endurance for the herald of the gospel carries eternity in their message.

The Evangelist's Cross:

1. What does the Greek word euangelion mean, and why does its meaning matter for understanding the essence of evangelism?

_____

_____

_____

2. In Acts 8, persecution scattered the church and launched Philip's ministry in Samaria. What does this reveal about the relationship between hardship and gospel expansion?

_____

_____

_____

3. Scenario: You are sent to preach in a culture with little to no exposure to Scripture. How would you faithfully present the gospel beginning from creation to Christ?

_____

_____

_____

4. Scenario: A skeptic says, "All religions lead to the same God." Using Scripture, how would you respond with both clarity and compassion?

_____

_____

_____

5. Which five Scriptures would you choose as your foundation to explain salvation to someone with no church background, and why?

_____

_____

_____

6. What role does the Holy Spirit play in both empowering the evangelist and convicting the hearer? Why is dependence on the Spirit essential?

_____

_____

_____

7. Why is personal holiness critical to an evangelist's credibility and fruitfulness? Support your answer with Scripture.

_____

_____

_____

Personal Challenge: If God called you today to leave comfort and proclaim Christ in a hostile or unfamiliar environment, how would you prepare spiritually, mentally, and practically?

_____

_____

_____

_____

_____

Final Commission

The evangelist stands at the edge of eternity, calling souls to step into the kingdom of God. Their work is hard, often lonely, and always opposed by darkness. But it is also the most vital work of all: without evangelism, the church loses its mission.

If you are preparing to step into this office, embrace the call with courage. Let the Spirit guide you, let Scripture ground you, and let compassion drive you. When you proclaim Christ, you are not just delivering words, more importantly you are carrying the eternal heartbeat of heaven into a lost and dying world.

"How, then, can they call on the one they have not believed in? And how can they believe in the one of

whom they have not heard? And how can they hear without someone preaching to them? And how can anyone preach unless they are sent? As it is written: "How beautiful are the feet of those who bring good news!" Romans 10:14–15

Conclusion: From Chaos to Calling

If you have made it through these pages, you have journeyed through the roles of servant, messenger, shepherd, and herald. You have seen how deacons model humility in service, how ministers carry the Word with diligence, how elders guard the flock with wisdom, and how evangelists compel the lost with urgency.

The truth is that ministry will always carry an element of chaos. The needs of people are endless, the weight of leadership is heavy, and the opposition from the enemy is real. But in the middle of that chaos stands the God who calls, equips, and sustains.

Remember this: the office does not make the person; the calling and character do. Titles may come and go, but what endures is a heart surrendered to God and a life willing to serve.

As you step into your next chapter of ministry, may you find peace in the process, strength in the Spirit, and joy in knowing that your labor in the Lord is never in vain. And may you never lose sight of the One who called you who is Jesus Christ, the Chief Shepherd, the Great Evangelist, and the Servant-King.

So go forth and serve faithfully, preach boldly, guard wisely, and evangelize passionately. The chaos of catechism is only the beginning of a lifelong journey of faith, leadership, and true transformation.

Glossary of Ministry Terms

Anointing:

The empowering presence of the Holy Spirit for a specific task or calling (1 Samuel 16:13; Acts 10:38).

Apostle (ἀπόστολος):

"One who is sent." Refers to those commissioned by Christ to establish churches, carry authority, and spread the gospel (Ephesians 4:11).

Bishop (ἐπίσκοπος):

Literally "overseer." A title often used interchangeably with elder, emphasizing responsibility for supervising doctrine, discipline, and care of the church (1 Tim. 3:1).

Calling:

The divine summons by which God sets apart individuals for specific work in His kingdom (Jeremiah 1:5; 2 Timothy 1:9).

Commission (Great Commission):

Christ's command to His followers to make disciples of all nations, baptizing and teaching them (Matthew 28:19–20).

Deacon (διάκονος):

Literally "servant" or "minister." A deacon is appointed to meet practical needs in the church, ensuring unity and care for all members (Acts 6).

Disciple:

A learner or follower of Jesus who submits to His teaching and example (Luke 9:23).

Elder (πρεσβύτερος):

Also "overseer" or "presbyter." Elders provide spiritual oversight, guidance, and shepherding for the local church.

Evangelist (εὐαγγελιστής):

A bearer of good news; one called to proclaim the gospel beyond the local congregation, often with a focus on outreach and mission.

Five-Fold Ministry:

Apostles, prophets, evangelists, pastors, and teachers which are given "for the equipping of the saints" (Ephesians 4:11–12).

Laying on of Hands:

A biblical practice for imparting blessing, healing, or ordination, symbolizing transfer of spiritual authority (Acts 6:6; 1 Tim. 4:14).

Martyr (μάρτυς):

Literally "witness." Refers to those who give their lives for the faith, with Stephen recognized as the first Christian martyr.

Minister (διάκονος / λειτουργός):

Broad term for one who serves God and the church through Word, sacraments, and acts of service.

Ordination:

The formal recognition and setting apart of individuals for ministry roles through prayer and the laying on of hands.

Preacher:

One who proclaims the Word of God with authority and clarity (Romans 10:14–15).

Servant Leadership:

A model patterned after Christ, who came "not to be served, but to serve" (Mark 10:45). It emphasizes humility and sacrifice.

Sheepfold:

A biblical metaphor for the gathered people of God, cared for by Christ the Good Shepherd (John 10:16).

Shepherd (ποιμήν):

Spiritual leaders who tend the flock of God with care, protection, and guidance (John 10; 1 Peter 5:2).

Stewardship:

The responsibility of managing God's resources, time, talent, and treasure faithfully and wisely (1 Corinthians 4:2).

Unity of the Body:

The church as one body with many members, functioning together in harmony under Christ the Head (1 Cor. 12:12–27).

Apostolic Succession:

The belief and practice that ecclesiastical authority is passed down through an unbroken chain of ordination, beginning with the apostles. Different traditions define and defend this concept uniquely.

Diakonia (Greek):

The New Testament term for service or ministry, is often applied to deacons. Goes beyond "helping" it implies a sacred stewardship of care, sacrifice, and practical love.

Presbyteros (Greek):

Translated as "elder," but connotes wisdom, maturity, and spiritual oversight. One who raises questions about governance, authority, and communal discernment in the church.

Charismata (Greek):

Spiritual gifts are given by the Holy Spirit for the building up of the body. A word that sparks debates on cessationism vs. continuationism, and the diversity of roles in ministry.

Exegesis vs. Eisegesis:

Two methods of biblical interpretation: exegesis draws meaning out of the text in its context, while eisegesis reads meaning into the text. Essential for preachers to grasp.

Ecclesiology:

The study of the church's nature, structure, mission, and identity. Challenges leaders to define what "church" really is institution, body, community, or kingdom movement.

Heresy vs. Orthodoxy:

"Heresy" (from hairesis, choice) refers to teachings outside accepted belief, while "orthodoxy" (right belief) reflects historic consensus. This tension has shaped church councils and leadership boundaries.

Kerygma (Greek):

The proclamation of the gospel message. More than a sermon but it is the very act of heralding Christ's death, burial, and resurrection as truth.

Sacerdotalism:

The idea that clergy serve as mediators of divine grace (especially through sacraments). Raises the question of priesthood vs. the "priesthood of all believers."

Anamnesis (Greek):

A remembrance that makes past events present often used in connection with the Lord's Supper. Ministry involves bringing the eternal into the now.

Syncretism:

The blending of Christianity with cultural or pagan practices in ways that compromise faith. Ministers must discern between contextualization and corruption.

Kenosis (Greek):

"Self-emptying" as described in Philippians 2:7. A model for ministers and deacons who must humble themselves for God's work.

Missio Dei (Latin):

"The mission of God" the understanding that ministry is not primarily the church's initiative, but God's own sending of His people into the world.

Catechism:

A structured set of questions and answers used to teach foundational doctrines of the faith.

Ecclesiology:

The theological study of the church, its structure, mission, and purpose.

Exegesis:

Careful interpretation of Scripture, drawing meaning out of the biblical text in its original context.

Hermeneutics:

The broader theory and method of interpreting Scripture and applying it to modern life.

Theophany:

A visible manifestation of God to humanity, such as the burning bush or cloud of glory.

Ecumenism:

The pursuit of unity among different Christian denominations and traditions.

Pastoral Epistles:

New Testament letters (1 & 2 Timothy, Titus) that outline pastoral care and leadership.

Missiology:

The study of the mission of the church, particularly evangelism and cross-cultural outreach.

Sanctification:

The ongoing process of being made holy and conformed to the image of Christ.

Christocentric Hermeneutic:

An interpretive approach that views all scripture both Old and New Testaments through a lense of Christ's person and work. That every biblical narrative points to Jesus as the fulfillment of God's redemptive story.

Ministry Readiness Exam

Section I: Multiple Choice Questions

Q1. What is Salvation?

a) Primarily moral self-improvement achieved through discipline

b) Deliverance from sin and reconciliation with God through Christ's atoning work

c) Entrance into church membership and adherence to traditions

d) An emotional religious experience without lasting transformation

Q2. Which best defines justification?

a) The lifelong process of becoming holy

b) God's legal declaration that a sinner is righteous through faith in Christ

c) The believer's personal effort to obey God's law

d) A temporary covering of sin until perfection is achieved

Q3. How does the New Testament describe saving faith?

a) Mental agreement with Christian doctrine

b) Belief that Jesus existed as a historical figure

c) Trust, reliance, and obedience directed toward Christ alone

d) A strong hope that one's good works will outweigh bad works

Q4. What is the Gospel at its core?

a) Advice for living a moral life

b) Good news that God saves sinners through the life, death, and resurrection of Jesus Christ

c) A collection of religious teachings passed down by the apostles

d) A call for humanity to reform society through justice and ethics alone

Q5. Why is grace essential for ministry?

a) It allows ministers to excuse personal failures without accountability

b) It equips and empowers believers for service beyond human ability

c) It replaces the need for prayer and discipline

d) It is earned through faithful attendance and service

Q6. According to Scripture, what is the evidence of genuine conversion?

a) Regular church attendance and service in a ministry role

b) Outward displays of enthusiasm during worship

c) The fruit of the Spirit and a transformed life that bears lasting fruit

d) Memorization of key Bible verses

Q7. Which statement best captures the biblical view of calling into ministry?

a) A career choice made after seminary

b) A divine summons confirmed by both inner conviction and external affirmation

c) A volunteer opportunity available to anyone who desires influence

d) An inherited right passed down through family tradition

Q8. In Ephesians 4:11–12, what is the primary purpose of ministers?

a) To control the direction of the church

b) To equip the saints for the work of ministry and build up the body of Christ

c) To carry the entire burden of spiritual growth for others

d) To ensure the church adapts to cultural trends

Q9. Why must ministers remain Spirit-led in their preaching and service?

a) So they can produce emotional responses in their listeners

b) Because human wisdom cannot accomplish spiritual transformation

c) To validate their authority before other leaders

d) To guarantee popularity and ministry success

Q10. Which danger most threatens those newly entering ministry?

a) Overdependence on Scripture

b) Reliance on human ability and neglect of private devotion

c) Seeking mentorship and accountability

d) Growing in humility and patience

Q11. According to Ephesians 4:11–12, the role of the evangelist is primarily:

a) To oversee church finances

b) To equip the saints for ministry

c) To replace the pastor when absent

d) To conduct worship services

Q12. The Greek term presbyteros is most closely translated as:

a) Teacher

b) Elder

c) Shepherd

d) Servant

Q13. In Acts 6, the appointment of the first deacons demonstrates what principle?

a) Leaders should avoid prayer to focus on logistics

b) Delegation allows the Word of God to spread without hindrance

c) Deacons are primarily responsible for preaching

d) Apostles are not accountable to the community

Q14. Which of these best describes "exegesis"?

a) Reading meaning into the text

b) Drawing meaning out of the text in context

c) Ignoring historical background

d) Relying only on tradition for interpretation

Q15. Spiritual pride is most dangerous in ministry because:

a) It makes leaders tired

b) It blinds leaders to correction and accountability

c) It reduces preaching effectiveness

d) It causes doctrinal debates

Section II:

Open-Ended (Reflection & Application)

1. Describe a time when you had to serve in humility. How did that shape your understanding of ministry?

_____

_____

_____

2. How should an evangelist remain both Bible-centered and Spirit-led?

_____

_____

_____

3. What safeguards can a leader establish to prevent burnout while staying effective in ministry?

_____

_____

_____

4. Compare the roles of a pastor and an evangelist. Why must they work together for a healthy church?

_____

_____

_____

Section III: Case Study/Scenario

Scenario 1:

You are asked to preach at a revival, but you notice a conflict among church leaders. How would you balance preparing your message with addressing the division?

_____

_____

_____

_____

Scenario 2:

A new believer comes to you struggling with doubt about their calling. What biblical and practical steps would you use to guide them?

_____

_____

_____

_____

Multiple Choice Questions:

Q1. According to 2 Timothy 2:15, a minister must:

a) Be prepared to debate anyone

b) Study to rightly divide the Word of Truth

c) Follow personal opinions

d) Depend on tradition alone

Q2. Which is most important for someone entering ministry?

a) A strong social media presence

b) A servant's heart

c) A large congregation

d) A charismatic personality

Q3. Jesus said in John 15:5, "Without Me you can do nothing." What does this teach ministers?

a) Ministry success depends on human effort

b) Fruitfulness flows from abiding in Christ

c) Spiritual gifts are unnecessary

d) Leadership is about independence

Q4. Which of the following is a danger for new ministers?

a) Spiritual pride

b) Humility

c) Accountability

d) Dependence on God

Q5. In Acts 6, the apostles appointed deacons because:

a) They wanted to avoid prayer

b) They wanted to focus on the Word and prayer

c) They needed someone to preach in their place

d) They did not care for the widows

Q6. The foundation of every sermon should be:

a) Personal stories

b) Cultural trends

c) The Word of God

d) Opinions of others

Q7. A minister's effectiveness is most hindered when they:

a) Pray daily

b) Walk in obedience

c) Neglect private devotion

d) Serve humbly

Q8. According to Galatians 5:22-23, the fruit of the Spirit demonstrates:

a) The true character of a minister

b) The ability to lead worship

c) How to manage finances

d) The gift of leadership

Q9. Why is accountability important for those entering ministry?

a) It limits creativity

b) It helps protect integrity and growth

c) It shows weakness

d) It is optional

Q10. The Great Commission (Matthew 28:19–20) commands ministers to:

a) Stay in one place and build a platform

b) Go and make disciples of all nations

c) Focus only on their local church

d) Preach without teaching

Q11. A leader who is Bible-centered demonstrates:

a) Reliance on human tradition

b) Commitment to sound doctrine

c) Freedom to misinterpret Scripture

d) Lack of structure in preaching

Q12. What is the role of prayer in ministry?

a) Optional preparation

b) The backbone of spiritual power and direction

c) A religious ritual only

d) Something left for intercessors

Q13. What does the term ecclesiology refer to?

a) The study of angels and demons

b) The study of the nature, mission, and function of the church

c) The study of personal holiness and devotion

d) The study of ancient biblical languages

Q14. In Acts 6, the apostles appointed deacons to oversee daily food distribution. What leadership principle does this decision highlight?

a) Practical service is less spiritual than preaching

b) Delegation preserves leaders' focus on prayer and the Word

c) Spiritual authority rests only with apostles

d) Leadership should remain centralized

Q15. According to 1 Timothy 3, why is managing one's household essential for ministry leadership?

a) It demonstrates organizational ability

b) It links integrity at home with credibility in the church

c) It ensures financial stability

d) It proves capability in teaching

Q16. Which truth best reflects Stephen's example in Acts 6–7?

a) Service is secondary to preaching

b) Faithfulness in service can lead to costly witness

c) Boldness always prevents persecution

d) Evangelism depends on cultural similarity

Q17. According to Titus 1:5-9, which qualification for elders is emphasized most?

a) Administrative competence

b) Speaking ability

c) Character and integrity

d) Strategic leadership skills

Q18. What primary danger did Paul warn about in Acts 20:28-31 when addressing elders?

a) Financial mismanagement

b) False teachers arising from inside and outside the church

c) Political interference in the church

d) Decline of community programs

Q19. Timothy's relationship with Paul illustrates which leadership principle?

a) Authority without accountability

b) Mentorship shapes ministry effectiveness

c) Ministers should work alone to prove maturity

d) Youth is a disqualification for leadership

Q20. Philip's encounter with the Ethiopian eunuch in Acts 8 teaches what evangelistic truth?

a) Evangelism requires large crowds for impact

b) Spirit-led obedience can transform even one life

c) Conversion must always happen in public worship

d) Evangelism depends primarily on cultural similarity

Q21. What best explains the difference between elders and deacons in the New Testament?

a) Elders serve practically; deacons serve spiritually

b) Elders shepherd and oversee; deacons serve and support

c) Deacons preach exclusively; elders manage finances

d) Elders lead services; deacons collect offerings

Q22. According to 2 Timothy 4:5, which responsibility is not explicitly listed for the evangelist?

a) Keep your head in all situations

b) Endure hardship

c) Perform signs and wonders

d) Do the work of an evangelist

Q23. What was the main issue addressed at the Council of Nicaea (AD 325)?

a) The canon of Scripture

b) The divinity of Christ

c) Baptism practices

d) The doctrine of justification by faith

Q24. Which New Testament book most emphasizes faith and works together, declaring, "Faith without works is dead"?

a) Romans

b) Galatians

c) James

d) Hebrews

Q25. The Hebrew word shalom means more than "peace." Which fuller meaning is correct?

a) Silence and stillness

b) Completeness, wholeness, well-being

c) Rest from enemies

d) Absence of war

Q26. Who is considered the "father of church history" for writing Ecclesiastical History in the 4th century?

a) Augustine

b) Athanasius

c) Eusebius

d) Tertullian

Q27. In Matthew 16:18, Jesus said, "Upon this rock I will build my church." Which Greek word for "rock" is used?

a) Petra

b) Lithos

c) Akrogōniaios

d) Chalix

Q28. According to Romans 5:1, believers are justified by faith and therefore have what?

a) Access to angels

b) Wealth and prosperity

c) Peace with God

d) Freedom from suffering

Q29. Which early reformer nailed his Ninety-Five Theses to the church door in Wittenberg in 1517?

a) John Calvin

b) Martin Luther

c) Ulrich Zwingli

d) John Wycliffe

Q30. Which Old Testament book contains the prophecy of the "Suffering Servant"?

a) Isaiah

b) Jeremiah

c) Psalms

d) Micah

Q31. The doctrine of the Trinity affirms that:

a) God reveals Himself in three roles but is one person

b) The Father, Son, and Spirit are three distinct persons, one essence

c) Jesus and the Spirit were created by the Father

d) God appears in three modes depending on the situation

Q32. The Dead Sea Scrolls, discovered in the 20th century, are most significant because they:

a) Contain early Christian writings

b) Preserve some of the oldest copies of Old Testament texts

c) Prove that Paul wrote all 13 epistles

d) Include lost gospels later added to the canon

Q33. In Acts 17, Paul preached at the Areopagus in Athens. What central theme did he use to connect with his Greek audience?

a) Israel's history

b) The "unknown god" they already worshiped

c) Roman law and order

d) Prophecies from Daniel

Q34. Which church father strongly opposed Arianism and defended the full divinity of Christ?

a) Augustine

b) Athanasius

c) Jerome

d) Origen

Q35. Which New Testament epistle contains the "Hall of Faith" (a list of Old Testament figures commended for their faith)?

a) Hebrews

b) Romans

c) James

d) Philippians

Q36. In John 1, Jesus is called the Logos. What does this Greek term mean?

a) Word

b) Life

c) Light

d) Teacher

Q37. Scenario: A member of your church insists baptism teaches that salvation comes by grace through faith, not works. Which passage best supports this truth?

a) John 3:16

b) Romans 10:9

c) Ephesians 2:8–9

d) Galatians 5:22

Q38. In Genesis 50:20, Joseph told his brothers, "You meant evil against me, but God meant it for good." This verse illustrates which doctrine?

a) Divine providence

b) Human free will

c) Justification by faith

d) The fall of man

Q39. In the Sermon on the Mount, Jesus said, "Blessed are the pure in heart..." How does He complete this beatitude?

a) "...for they shall inherit the earth."

b) "...for they shall see God."

c) "...for they shall be comforted."

d) "...for theirs is the kingdom of heaven."

Q40. Which New Testament letter contains the "armor of God" passage?

a) Colossians

b) Ephesians

c) 1 Thessalonians

d) Philippians

Q41. Which early church father translated the Bible into Latin (the Vulgate)?

a) Augustine

b) Jerome

c) Origen

d) Polycarp

Q42. The doctrine of justification by faith alone was most strongly emphasized during which historical movement?

a) The Crusades

b) The Reformation

c) The Great Schism

d) The Enlightenment

Q43. In Acts 5, Ananias and Sapphira were judged for:

a) Refusing to sell their land

b) Withholding money while lying about their gift

c) Criticizing Peter publicly

d) Neglecting the widows

Q44. Scenario: You are discipling a new believer who struggles to understand assurance of salvation. Which passage most directly teaches security in Christ?

a) Psalm 23:1

b) John 10:28–29

c) Galatians 2:20

d) Romans 12:1

Q45. The Council of Chalcedon (AD 451) clarified which doctrine?

a) The dual nature of Christ — fully God and fully man

b) The authority of the pope

c) Baptism by immersion only

d) Predestination

Q46. In John 15, Jesus describes Himself as the "true vine." What is required of the branches to bear fruit?

a) Pruning through hardship

b) Abiding in Him

c) Producing works on their own

d) Avoiding persecution

Q47. According to Romans 8:26, how does the Holy Spirit help believers in prayer?

a) By teaching eloquent words

b) By interceding with groans too deep for words

c) By reminding them of Old Testament laws

d) By replacing prayer altogether

Q48. Which Old Testament figure first received the covenant sign of circumcision?

a) Noah

b) Moses

c) Abraham

d) Isaiah

Q49. A believer insists that since they are saved by grace, obedience no longer matters. Which passage most directly corrects this misunderstanding?

a) Romans 6:1–2

b) Ephesians 6:10–18

c) John 3:16

d) Matthew 28:19

Q50. In Philippians 2, Paul describes Christ's humility. Which phrase captures His willingness to take on humanity?

a) "Made in the image of God"

b) "Formed in the likeness of Adam"

c) "Made Himself nothing, taking the very nature of a servant"

d) "Became greater than angels"

Q51. What is sectarianism in a Christian context?

a) The belief that all religions ultimately lead to God

b) Excessive attachment to a particular group or denomination, causing division in the Body of Christ

c) The pursuit of holiness through separation from worldly activities

d) The rejection of church authority in favor of personal spirituality

Q52. What does the term soteriology refer to?

a) The study of the end times

b) The study of salvation and how it is accomplished

c) The study of church governance

d) The study of spiritual gifts

Q53. In Christian theology, what is the danger of syncretism?

a) Believing God exists as three persons in one essence

b) Blending biblical faith with non-Christian religions or cultural practices in a way that compromises truth

c) Dividing the church into clergy and laity

d) Elevating tradition above Scripture

Q54. What is the primary purpose of the fruit of the Spirit in the life of a believer?

a) To prove one's salvation before others

b) To demonstrate the Spirit's sanctifying work by shaping the believer's character into Christlikeness

c) To guarantee success in ministry and leadership

d) To serve as outward evidence of spiritual gifts

Q55. Why is the doctrine of the Resurrection essential to Christian ministry?

a) It proves that Jesus was greater than the Old Testament prophets

b) It validates Christ's victory over sin and death, providing the foundation for hope and eternal life

c) It serves only as a symbolic metaphor for spiritual renewal

d) It guarantees believers will never experience physical suffering

NOTES

_____

_____

_____

_____

_____

_____

Q56. What is faith, and why is it important?

a) Faith is blind optimism; it matters because it keeps people emotionally stable.

b) Faith is confidence in God's character and promises; it is important because without it, impossibility is present.

c) Faith is human effort to remain morally pure; it matters because it earns salvation.

d) Faith is intellectual agreement with religious doctrine; it is important because it ensures correct knowledge of Scripture.

NOTES

_____

_____

_____

_____

_____

_____

Q57. What was Isaiah's role in heralding the coming of Christ?

a) Isaiah functioned as a political reformer; his message about a Messiah was metaphorical and limited to Israel's kings.

b) His prophecies identified Christ as the Suffering Servant and Immanuel, offering a royal and redemptive portrait pointing to incarnation and atonement.

c) Isaiah spoke of a Messiah only as a military leader, predicting a national liberator rather than a spiritual savior.

d) Isaiah's role was minimal; the coming of Christ was heralded exclusively by John the Baptist in the New Testament.

REFLECTIONS

_____

_____

_____

_____

_____

Q58. What is the meaning of the Fruit of the Spirit?

a) They are natural human virtues that anyone can develop through discipline and positive thinking.

b) They are supernatural qualities produced by the Holy Spirit in believers, reflecting Christ's character and serving as evidence of spiritual maturity and transformation.

c) They are symbolic descriptions of Israel's agricultural blessings, with no application for Christians today.

d) They are external works performed to prove salvation and earn God's approval.

NOTES

_____

_____

_____

_____

_____

_____

Q59. What is the relationship between grace and the law in Christian theology?

a) Grace cancels the law completely, leaving believers without moral framework.

b) Grace is God's unearned favor that fulfills what the law pointed to; the law reveals humanity's need for salvation, while grace provides it through Christ (Rom 6:14; Gal 3:24).

c) The law and grace are equal paths to salvation, and believers can choose either.

d) Grace applies only to Gentiles, while the law remains the binding covenant for all believers.

REFLECTIONS

_____

_____

_____

_____

_____

_____

Q60. What is the significance of the Cross, Death, Burial, and Resurrection of Christ?

a) They symbolize human suffering and resilience, encouraging believers to endure hardship.

b) They are the central act of redemption — revealing God's love and justice, securing atonement for sin, confirming Christ's humanity, and demonstrating His victory over death (1 Cor 15:3).

c) They are historical events with limited spiritual meaning, pointing to Jesus as a moral example.

d) They serve as church traditions remembered during Easter but hold no continuing relevance for us today.

NOTES

_____

_____

_____

_____

_____

_____

Open-Ended Questions:

1. What does it mean to "shepherd the flock of God" (1 Peter 5:2), and how can a pastor do this without lording over people?

_____

_____

_____

2. Explain the biblical and theological significance of baptism. Why is it more than just a ritual, and what dangers come if the church treats it lightly?

_____

_____

_____

3. Why is the cross not just the starting point of salvation, but the ongoing pattern for Christian ministry?

_____

_____

_____

Prayer & Ministry
Journal Starter

Prompts:

1. Write out a prayer for your family, ministry, or calling.

_____

_____

_____

_____

_____

_____

2. **What do you desire to see God do through your ministry in the next 5 years?**

_____

_____

_____

_____

_____

_____

_____

_____

_____

_____

_____

_____

_____

_____

3. **What weaknesses do you want God to strengthen as you grow?**

_____

_____

_____

_____

_____

_____

_____

_____

_____

_____

_____

_____

_____

_____

_____

_____

Recommended Resources

1. *Spiritual Leadership by J. Oswald Sanders*

2. *The Making of a Leader by Frank Damazio*

3. *Biblical Eldership by Alexander Strauch*

4. *The Amazing Weight by Marissa Farrow*

5. *The Master Plan of Evangelism by Robert E. Coleman*

6. *Disciples Are Made, Not Born by Walter A. Henrichsen, Everyday Evangelism by Preston Perry*

7. *UrbanLogia Ministries (YouTube) Damon Richardson*

Final Notes:

A space for your reflections, learnings, and next steps as you continue in your ministry journey.

Use this area to record key insights from your preparation, commitments you are making to God, or lessons you want to carry with you into your service.

_____

_____

_____

_____

_____

_____

_____

_____